SPECIAL REPORT

AGENDA 21 &

HOW TO STOP IT

TOM DEWEESE

PRODUCED BY:

AMERICAN POLICY CENTER

ISBN 9781790653522 (Paperback)
1.6, July 2019

Special thanks to Commissioner Richard Rothschild
who designed many of graphics in this booklet

To download or order copies of this booklet visit:
americanpolicy.org

ABOUT THE AMERICAN POLICY CENTER

The American Policy Center (APC), located in suburban Washington, D.C., is a privately funded, nonprofit, 501 c (4), tax-exempt grassroots action and education foundation dedicated to the promotion of free enterprise and limited government regulations over commerce and individuals.

APC believes that the free market, through its inherent system of checks and balances, including private ownership of property, is the best method yet devised for creating individual wealth, full employment, goods and services, and protecting the natural environment.

APC's approach to establishing free market policy is rooted in the conviction that a well-informed American public is the best guarantee that U.S. policy will be guided by a keen awareness of the complexity of world politics and America's role in it.

To these ends, the American Policy Center has developed a wide range of programs designed to enhance national awareness of crucial global and domestic developments. In particular, APC focuses on the issues of environmental policy and its effect on private property rights; national federal computer data banks and their effect on individual privacy rights; the United Nations and its effect on American national sovereignty; and federal education policy and its effect on local schools and parental rights.

To promote its positions, APC publishes The DeWeese Report and occasionally special reports. Both are available through subscription. In addition, APC principals regularly appear on radio and television talk shows, and speak publicly before local and national conferences.

The American Policy Center is one of the nation's leading grassroots activist organizations. Its action alert system, Sledgehammer, mobilizes thousands of activists through fax and e-mail when legislative action is required. Regular legislative updates are issued bi-weekly through the APC Newswire.

As a result of its legislative activity, contributions to the American Policy Center are not tax-deductible. APC is funded primarily from small, individual contributions of its supporters and occasional grants from private foundations and businesses. APC does not accept government grants of any kind.

SUSTAINABLE DEVELOPMENT: THE TRANSFORMATION OF AMERICA

BY TOM DEWEESE

Some think that the planet is in danger of global warming and over consumption. They really believe that the only way to fix the problem is to control the flow of resources and wealth, which literally means changing human civilization and the way we live. The problem is, that requires a forced transformation of our entire society to comply, and that ultimately leads to a thirst for power and top-down control – that will eventually lead to tyranny.

In his book, Earth in the Balance, Al Gore warned that a "wrenching transformation" must take place to lead America away from the "horrors of the Industrial Revolution." The process to do that is called Sustainable Development and its' roots can be traced back to a UN policy document called Agenda 21, adopted at the UN's Earth Summit in 1992.

Sustainable Development calls for changing the very infrastructure of the nation, away from private ownership and control of property to nothing short of central planning of the entire economy – often referred to as top-down control.

WHERE AND WHEN DID THE TERM SUSTAINABLE DEVELOPMENT ORIGINATE?

The term "sustainable development" was born in the pages of "Our Common Future," the official report of the 1987 United Nations World Commission on Environment and Development,

authored by Gro Harlem Brundtland, Vice President of the
World Socialist Party. For the first time the environment was
tied to the tried and true Socialist goals of international redistribution of wealth. Said the report, "Poverty is a major cause
and effect of global environmental problems. It is therefore
futile to attempt to deal with environmental problems without
a broader perspective that encompasses the factors underlying
world poverty and international inequality."

The term appeared in full force in 1992, in a United Nations ini-
tiative called the U.N. Sustainable Development Agenda 21, or
as it has become known around the world, simply Agenda 21. It
was unveiled at the 1992 United Nations Conference on Environment and Development (UNCED), ballyhooed as the Earth
Summit. In fact, the Earth Summit was one of the provisions
called for in the Brundtland report as a means of implementing Sustainable Development around the world. More than 178
nations adopted Agenda 21 as official policy. President George
H.W. Bush was the signatory for the United States.

WHAT IS SUSTAINABLE DEVELOPMENT?

The 1989 Webster's Dictionary defines "Sustainable Yield" as a
requirement that trees cut down in a forest area be replaced
by new plantings to ensure future lumber supplies." That's what
most people think Sustainable Development means. Proponents of Sustainable Development argue that it is about pre-
serving resources for future generations. What's wrong with
that? Nothing in theory. That would be sustainable with a small
"s." Just common sense usage of natural resources.

The problem is, major forces now promoting it intend for
Sustainable Development to be spelled with a capital "S." They
intend for a Socio-economic political movement that probes,
invades and changes every aspect of human civilization. And
that's the problem.

Imagine an America in which a specific "ruling principle" is
created to decide proper societal conduct for every citizen.
That principle would be used to consider regulations guiding

everything you eat, the kind of home you are allowed to live in, the method of transportation you use to get to work, what kind of work you may have, the way you dispose of waste, perhaps even the number of children you may have, as well as the quality and amount of education your children may receive. Sustainable development encompasses every aspect of our lives.

According to its authors, the objective of sustainable development is to integrate economic, social, and environmental policies in order to achieve reduced consumption, social equity, and the preservation and restoration of biodiversity.

TOP 10 SUSTAINABILITY FALLACIES

0   **Sustainability is about protecting the environment. REALITY: It's a political movement to replace capitalism with government control of everything**

1   **Free market capitalism is the principle cause of planetary degradation and is not sustainable.   REALITY: It is government centric control of the economy that is not sustainable**

2   **Private Property is a source of social injustice, and too valuable to be subject to free markets.   REALITY: The right to own and use private property is a fundamental source of wealth creation**

3   **Green Energy creates jobs. REALITY: Green energy is unreliable, uncompetitive and renders industry unable to compete in world markets**

4   **CO2 is a pollutant.   REALITY: CO2 is the air that all plants and crops breath. More CO2= Better ag production**

5   **The Sustainability Movement isn't trying to take away anyone's property rights or freedoms.   REALITY: The Sustainability movement is relentlessly attacking property rights and freedoms**

6   **Climate change is catastrophic & anthropogenic and must be addressed through CO2 abatement schemes. REALITY: It is not catastrophic, and as a practical matter CO2 reductions WILL NOT WORK. You'll see NO CLAIMS of even 1/1000th a degree improvement. Washout time >100 yrs**

7   **Compact Development reduces pollution**
    REALITY: Dense development is always correlated with more intense pollution levels

8   **Subways and mass transit can replace cars.**
    REALITY: They can't. If they could, there'd be no cars in Manhattan.

9   **Compact Urban Development is more affordable for gov't**
    REALITY: Empirical evidence proves compact development requires higher tax rates. Urbanization strains police; fire, educational, and social services.

10 **Affordable Housing for people of ALL INCOME levels will ensure healthier better balanced neighborhoods. REALITY: Low income and Section-8 housing usually create more problems then they solve... thereby damaging communities**   5

The Sustainablists insist that society be transformed into feudal-like governance by making Nature the central organizing principle for our economy and society, not human need or wants. This idea essentially elevates nature above Man. As such, every societal decision would first be questioned as to how it might effect the environment. To achieve this, Sustainablist policy focuses on three components; land use, education, and population control and reduction.

Here is a direct quote from the report of the 1976 UN's Habitat I conference which said: "Land ...cannot be treated as an ordinary asset, controlled by individuals and subject to the pressures and inefficiencies of the market. Private land ownership is also a principle instrument of accumulation and concentration of wealth, therefore, contributes to social injustice."

Some officials claim that Sustainable Development is just a local effort to protect the environment and contain development -- just your local leaders putting together a local vision for the community. Yet, the exact language and tactics for implementation of Sustainable Development are being used in nearly every city around the globe from Lewiston, Maine to Singapore. Local indeed.

In short, Sustainable Development is the process by which America is being reorganized around a central principle of state collectivism using the environment as bait.

One of the best ways to understand what Sustainable Development actually is can be found by discovering what is NOT sustainable.

According to the UN's Biodiversity Assessment Report, items for our everyday lives that are NOT sustainable include: Ski runs, grazing of livestock, plowing of soil, building fences, industry, single family homes, paved and tarred roads, logging activities, dams and reservoirs, power line construction, and economic systems that fail to set proper value on the environment (capitalism, free markets).

Maurice Strong, Secretary General of the UN's Rio Earth Summit in 1992 said, "...Current lifestyles and consumption patterns of the affluent middle class – involving high meat intake, use of fossil fuels, appliances, home and work air-conditioning, and suburban housing are not sustainable."

This goal is exactly the policies that are written into such legislation as Cap and Trade, the Clean Air Act, the Clean Water Act. It is also the policy behind the many corporate commercials seen nightly on television which advocate "Going Green. They are all part of the efforts to modify American consumer behavior to accept less, deal with higher energy prices, restrict water use and place severe limitations on use of private property – all under the environmental excuse.

And one of the most destructive tools used to enforce Sustainable Development policy is something called the "precautionary principle." That means that any activities that might threaten human health or the environment should be stopped -- even if no clear cause and effect relationship has been established – and even if the potential threat is largely theoretical.

That makes it easy for any activist group to issue concerns or warnings by news release or questionable report against and industry or private activity, and have those warnings quickly turned into public policy – just in case.

Many are now finding non-elected regional governments and governing councils enforcing policy and regulations. As these policies are implemented, locally-elected officials are actually losing their own power and decision-making ability in their elected offices. More and more decisions are now being made behind the scenes in non-elected "sustainability councils" armed with truckloads of federal regulations, guidelines, and grant money.

THE THREE ES

According to its authors, the objective of Sustainable Development is to integrate economic, social, and environmental policies in order to achieve reduced consumption, social equity, and the preservation and restoration of biodiversity.

The Sustainable Development logo used in most literature on the subject contains three connecting circles labeled Social Equity; Economic Prosperity; and Ecological Integrity (known commonly as the 3 Es).

SOCIAL EQUITY

Sustainable Development's Social Equity plank is based on a demand for "social justice." Social Justice is described as the right and opportunity of all people "to benefit equally from the resources afforded us by society and the environment." According to Sustainablist doctrine, it is a social injustice for some to have prosperity if others do not. It is a social injustice to keep our borders closed. It is a social injustice for some to be bosses and others to be merely workers. Social justice is a major premise of Sustainable Development. Another word for social justice is Socialism or Marxism. Karl Marx was the first to coin the phrase "social justice."

Most recently the theory of social justice has been used to justify government takeover of health care. Today, the phrase is used throughout Sustainablist literature. The Sustainablist system is based on the principle that individuals must give up selfish wants for the needs of the common good, or the "community."

This is the same policy behind the push to eliminate our nation's borders to allow the "migration" of those from other nations into the United States to share our individually-created wealth and our taxpayers-paid government social programs. Say the Sustainablists, "Justice and efficiency go hand in hand." "Borders," they say, "are unjust."

Under the Sustainablist system, private property is an evil that is used simply to create wealth for a few. So too, is business ownership. Instead, "every worker/person will be a direct capital owner." Property and businesses are to be kept in the name of the owner, keeping them responsible for taxes and other expenses, however control is in the hands of the "community" (government).

Under Sustainable Development individual human wants, needs, and desires are to be conformed to the views and dictates of social planners. Harvey Ruvin, Vice Chair of the International Council on Local Environmental Initiatives (ICLEI) said: "individual rights will have to take a back seat to the collective" in the process of implementing Sustainable Development.

ECONOMIC PROSPERITY

Sustainable Development's economic policy is based on one overriding premise: that the wealth of the world was made at the expense of the poor. It dictates that, if the conditions of the poor are to be improved, wealth must first be taken from the rich. Consequently, Sustainable Development's economic policy is based, not on private enterprise, but on public/private partnerships.

In America's free-market of the past, most businesses were started by individuals who saw a need for a product or service and they set out to fill it. Some businesses prospered to become huge corporations, some remained small "mom and pop" shops, others failed and dissolved. Most business owners were happy to be left alone to take their chances to run their businesses on their own, not encumbered by a multiplicity of government regulations. If they failed, most found a way to try again. In the beginning of the American Republic, government's main involvement was to guarantee they had the opportunity to try.

In order to give themselves an advantage over competition, some businesses -- particularly large corporations – now find a great advantage in dealing directly with government, actively lobbying for legislation that will inundate smaller companies with regulations that they cannot possibly comply with or even keep up with. This government/big corporation back-scratching has always been a dangerous practice because economic power should be a positive check on government power, and vise versa. If the two should ever become combined, control of such massive power can lead only to tyranny. One of the best examples of this was the Italian model in the first half of the Twentieth Century under Mussolini's Fascism.

Together, select business leaders who have agreed to help government impose Sustainablist green positions in their business policies, and officials at all levels of government are indeed merging the power of the economy with the force of government in Public/Private Partnerships on the local, state and federal levels.

As a result, Sustainable Development policy is redefining free trade to mean centralized global trade "freely" crossing (or eliminating) national borders. It definitely does not mean people and companies trading freely with each other. Its real effect is to redistribute American manufacturing, wealth, and jobs out of our borders and to lock away American natural resources. After the regulations have been put in place, literally destroying whole industries, new "green" industries created with federal grants bring newfound wealth to the "partners." This is what Sustainablists refer to as economic prosperity.

The Sustainable Development "partnerships" include some corporations both domestic and multination. They in turn are partnered with the politicians who use their legislative and administrative powers to raid the treasury to fund and enforce the scheme.

Of course, as the chosen corporations, which become a new elite, stamp out the need for competition through government power, the real loser is the consumers who no longer count in market decisions. Government grants are now being used by industry to create mandated green products like wind and solar power. Products are put on the market at little risk to the industry, leaving consumers a more limited selection from which to choose. True free markets are eliminated in favor of controlled economies which dictate the availability and quality of products.

ECOLOGICAL INTEGRITY

"Nature has an integral set of different values (cultural, spiritual and material) where humans are one strand in nature's web and all living creatures are considered equal. Therefore the natural way is the right way and human activities should be molded along nature's rhythms." from the UN's Biodiversity Treaty presented at the 1992 UN Earth Summit.

This quote lays down the ground rules for the entire Sustainable Development agenda. It says humans are nothing special – just one strand in the nature of things or, put another way, humans are simply biological resources. Sustainablist policy is to oversee any issue in which man interacts with nature – which, of course, is literally everything. And because the environment always comes first, there must be great restrictions over private property ownership and control. This is necessary, Sustainablists say, because humans only defile nature.

Under Sustainable Development there can be no concern over individual rights. Individual human wants, needs, and desires are conformed to the views and dictates of social planners. The UN's Commission on Global Governance said in its 1995 report: "Human activity...combined with unprecedented increases in human numbers...are impinging on the planet's basic life support system. Action must be taken now to control the human activities that produce these risks"

Under Sustainable Development, limited government, as advocated by our Founding Fathers, is impossible because, we are told, the real or perceived environmental crisis is too great. Only government can be trusted to respond. Maurice Strong, Chairman of the 1992 UN Earth Summit said: "A shift is necessary toward lifestyles less geared to environmentally-damaging consumption patterns. The shift will require a vast strengthening of the multilateral system, including the United Nations."

The politically based environmental movement provides Sustainablists camouflage as they work to transform the American systems of government, justice, and economics. It is a masterful mixture of socialism (with its top down control of the tools of the economy) and fascism (where property is owned in name only – with no individual owner control). Sustainable Development is the worst of both the left and the right. It is not liberal, nor is it conservative. It is a new kind of tyranny that, if not stopped, will surely lead us to a new Dark Ages of pain and misery yet unknown to mankind.

UN report- Habitat I conference:

UN-HABITAT

- *"Land ... cannot be treated as an ordinary asset, controlled by individuals and subject to the pressures and inefficiencies of the market. Private land ownership is also a principle instrument of accumulation and concentration of wealth, therefore, contributes to social injustice."*

THE REINVENTION OF GOVERNMENT

Six months after his inauguration, President Bill Clinton issued Executive Order #12852 which created the President's Council On Sustainable Development (PCSD) on June 29 1993.

The Council's Membership included:
- Twelve Cabinet-level Federal Officials
- Jonathan Lash, Pres. World Resources Institute
- John Adams, Ex. Dir. National Resources Defense Council
- Dianne Dillon-Ridgley, Pres. Zero Population

• Michelle Perrault, International V.P., Sierra Club
• John C. Sawhill, Pres. The Nature Conservancy
• Jay D. Hair, Pres. World Conservation Union (IUCN)
• Kenneth L. Lay, CEO, Enon Corporation
• William D. Ruckelshaus, Chm., Browning-Ferris Industries & former EPA Administrator

Some of these members were representatives of the same groups which helped write Agenda 21 at the UN level, now openly serving on the President's Council to create policy for the implementation of Sustainable Development at the federal level
.

With great fanfare the Council issued a comprehensive report containing all the guidelines on how our government was to be reinvented under sustainable development. Those guidelines were created to direct policy for every single federal agency, state government and local community government.

Their purpose was to translate the recommendations set forth in Agenda 21 into public policy administered by the federal government. They created the American version of Agenda 21 called "Sustainable America - A New Consensus".

THE FOUR PART PROCESS LEADING TO SUSTAINABLE DEVELOPMENT

So how is this "wrenching transformation" being put into place? There are four very specific routes being used. In the rural areas it's called the "Wildlands Project." In the cities it's called "Smart Growth." In business it's called "Public/Private Partnerships." And in government it's called "Stakeholder Councils."

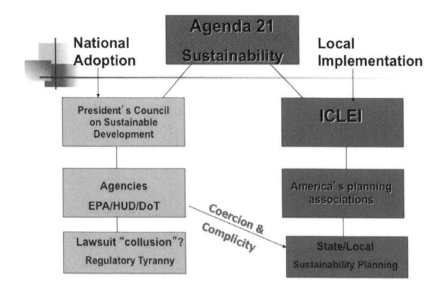

THE WILDLANDS PROJECT

"We must make this place an insecure and inhospitable place for capitalists and their projects... We must relcaim the roads and plowed lands, halt dam construction, tear down existing dams, free shackled rivers and return to wilderness millions of tens of millions of acres of presently settled land." - Dave Foremen, Earth First.

The Wildlands Project was the brainchild of Earth First's Dave Foreman and it literally calls for the "re-wilding" of 50% of all the land in every state – back to the way it was before Christopher Columbus set foot on this land.

It is a diabolical plan to herd humans off the rural lands and into human settlements. Crazy you say! Yes. Impossible? Not so fast. From Foreman, the plan became the blueprint for the UN's Biodiversity Treaty and quickly became international in scope.

But how do you remove people from the land? One step at a time. Let's begin with a biosphere reserve. A national park will do. A huge place where there is no human activity. For example, Yellowstone National Park, devoid of human habitation can serve as its center. Then a buffer zone is established around the reserve. Inside the buffer only limited human activity is allowed. Slowly, through strict regulations, that area is squeezed until human activity becomes impossible.

Once that is accomplished, the biosphere is extended to the former buffer zone borders – and then a new buffer zone is created around the now-larger biosphere and the process starts again. In that way, the Biosphere Reserve acts like a cancer cell, ever expanding, until all human activity is stopped.

And there are many tools in place to stop human activity and grow the reserve.

Push back livestock's access to river banks on ranches, many times as much as . 300. When the cattle can't reach the stream, the rancher can't water them -- he goes out of business. Lock away natural resources by creating national parks. It shuts down the mines -- and they go out of business. Invent a Spotted Owl shortage and pretend it can't live in a forest where timber is cut. Shut off the forest. Then, when no trees are cut, there's nothing to feed the mills and then there are no jobs, and -- they go out of business.

Locking away land cuts the tax base. Eventually the town dies. Keep it up and there is nothing to keep the people on the land – so they head to the cities. The wilderness grows – just like Dave Foreman planned.

It comes in many names and many programs. Heritage areas, land management, wolf and bear reintroduction, rails to trails, conservation easements, open space, and many more. Each of these programs is designed to make it just a little harder to live on the land – a little more expensive – a little more hopeless, literally herding people off their land and into designated human habitat areas – cities.

In the West, where vast areas of open space make it easy to impose such polices there are several programs underway to remove humans from the land. Today, there are at least 31 Wildlands projects underway, locking away more than 40 percent of the nation's land. The Alaska Wildlands Project seeks to lock away and control almost the entire state. In Washington State, Oregon, Idaho, Montana parts of North and South Dakota, parts of California, Arizona, Nevada, New Mexico, Wyoming, Texas, Utah, and more, there are at least 22 Wildlands Projects underway. For example, one project called Yukon to Yellowstone (Y2Y) – creates a 2000 mile no-man's land corridor from the Arctic to Yellowstone.

East of the Mississippi, there are at least nine Wildlands projects, covering Maine, Pennsylvania, New York, West Virginia, Ohio, Virginia, Tennessee, North and South Carolina, Georgia and Florida. Watch for names of Wildlands Projects like Chesapeake Bay Watershed, Appalachian Restoration Project and Piedmont Wildlands Project.

How did we get here?
J Gary Lawrence

- **Clinton's advisor for Sustainable Development:**

  *"Participating in a U.N. advocated planning process would very likely bring out many ... right wing conspiracy groups...who would actively work to defeat any elected official... undertaking Local Agenda 21. **So we call our process something else, such as "comprehensive planning," "growth management," or "smart growth."***

SMART GROWTH

The second path is called Smart Growth. The process essentially puts a line around a city, locking off any growth outside that line. Such growth is disdainfully labeled "Urban Sprawl."

The plan then curtails the building of more roads to cut off access to the newly created rural area. Inside the circle, concerted efforts are made to discourage the use of cars in preference to public transportation, restricting mobility.

Because there is a restriction on space inside the controlled city limits, there is a created shortage of land and houses, so prices go up. That means populations will have to be controlled, because now there is no room to contain more people.

Cities are now passing "green" regulations, forcing homeowners to meet strict guidelines for making their homes environmentally compliant, using specific building materials, forcing roof replacements, demanding replacement of appliances, and more. Those not in compliance will be fined and will not be able to sell their homes. There are now efforts underway to impose so-called "smart meters" which replace thermostats in homes. Homeowners will not have control of such meters. Instead, the electric company will determine the necessary temperature inside each home. Government agencies or local policy boards will be tasked with the responsibility to conduct an energy audit in each home to determine the steps necessary to bring the home into energy compliance. In Oakland, California, such restrictions will cost each homeowner an estimated $36,000.

The Cap N Trade bill contains a whole section on such restrictions for the nation, and most local communities are now busy creating development plans that encompass many of the same restrictions.

There is now a new push to control food production under the label of Sustainable Farming. Food sheds are now being advocated. These are essentially government run farms located just outside the smart growth area circling the city. Food is to be grown using strict guidelines which dictate what kinds of food is to be produced and the farming practices to be used. These are essentially based on the blue print of Chinese Agrarian villages that cannot possibly grow enough food to feed the community unless populations are tightly controlled. True Sustainable farming programs discourage importing goods from outside the community.

SMART GROWTH A DUMB DEAL FOR THE POOR

In 1880, he was noticeable. Dressed in long coat and top hat, his one hand wielded a magic wand punctuating the elixir in the other. His concoction cured all from headaches, to "kidney trouble."

Today's snake oiler is college educated, marketing savvy and lends an infectious passion to Smart Growth, the 21st Century solve-all. He and his slick supporters, claim to repair every-thing from jobs and climate change to social justice and traffic congestion, all while returning the environment to Hiawathan pristinity.

Unlike his 19th century counterpart, today's Smart Growth planner has wrought financial wreckage and shattered oppor-tunities across a landscape of American communities. Sleek rail trains, trimmed public parks and decoratively obstructed "calm" streets hide his customers' dashed hopes.

Once community members escape the trance of mixed-use ef-ficiency, granite counter tops and gleaming stainless applianc-es, once they realize the meandering bike path and community swing sets are mandates, not options, the wake-up is jolting.

As Smart Growth planning coaxes people out of single home suburban living and into boxed quarters near transit lines, parents soon realize the land their children play on is no longer theirs. Dad cannot build a backyard sandbox with his kids or spend the weekend constructing a new tree-house as a family project.

The economics of Smart Growth are sobering and hit few harder than the poor. As growth boundaries limit new home construction outside of the perimeters, concentrated con-struction within the defined area drives housing prices beyond the reach of most.

According to Wendell Cox, prior to the Smart Growth surge of the 1990's an average home cost just 2.5 to 3 times the median income of community residents. A person earning $40,000 annually could likely purchase a home for $120,000.

But, in 2006, in Smart Growth cities like Boston, Portland and San Diego, homes respectively cost 6, 5 and 10.5 times the median family income. Homes costing just 4 times or more annual income are considered "seriously unaffordable."

A family earning $125,000 in San Diego would be hard-pressed to afford a home 10 times that amount. Routinely, they shrink their living standards and move into ever smaller dwellings.

Housing costs in Seattle are so exorbitant; people are turning to renting and downsizing. The Wallingford Apartments offer 190 square feet of living space at a cost of $825 per month.

But the poor do not earn $125,000 or even half of that. So, what becomes of them under Smart Growth? Look no further than Portland, Oregon, heralded by the NYT as the epitome of prescriptive planning.

In the 1980's, Portland was one of the most diverse and affordable markets for single family homes in the country. By 1996, over 20 years of Smart Growth planning had taken its toll. Traffic congestion, housing shortages, increased home costs, higher taxes, costly rail transit and private backyards swapped for public open spaces created a picturesque visitors' paradise borne on the backs of the poor and middle class.

What was once a diverse city is now mockingly called the 'whitest city in America.' In spite of affordable housing programs and years of planner's good intentions, Portland has created a ring of poverty that has shoved poor blacks into low-income areas as the wealthy push them out of the city core. Then City Commissioner, Gretchen Kafoury said, "Oh my God!

We thought we were doing a good thing."

In San Francisco, 36% of poor black families living in "communities of concern," will be displaced to make way for transit-oriented communities. According to the Draft Environmental Impact Report, "displacement is a significant impact that cannot be mitigated."

The suffering of the poor under Smart Growth extends beyond housing. As community members pay rising mortgages and taxes, the middle class is dwindling. A 2013 study by the Center for American Progress shows that poor families rise out of poverty fastest when living in an area with a strong middle class. With the middle class in Smart Growth areas shrinking and housing costs rising, where does that leave the poor?

Call it Smart Growth, sustainable development or regionalism. To poor and low-income families, it is pure snake oil.

A **red agenda** marketed with pretty green name: "**sustainability**"

- **Agenda 21 spread like an INFECTION:**
  UN A21→ ICLEI → NGO's → State Planners
- America's planning association(s) provide sample ordinances based on ICLEI doctrine that originated in UN Agenda 21
- Municipal Plans become Manifestos.

STAKE HOLDER COUNCILS

Inside the cities, government is increasingly controlled by an elite ruling class called stake holder councils. These are mostly Non-governmental organizations, or NGOs, which, like thieves in the night, converge on the community to stake their claim to enforce their own private agendas. The function of legitimately – elected government within the system votes to create a system of boards, councils and even regional governments to handle every aspect of day-to-day operation of the community. Once in place, the councils and boards basically replace the power of elected officials with non-elected, appointed rulers answerable to no one.

The councils are controlled by a small minority in the community, but they are all- powerful. They force citizens to seek permission (usually denied) for any changes to private property. They use such excuses as historic preservation, water use restrictions, energy use, and open space restrictions. They will dictate that homeowners must use special "green" light bulbs and force stores to only use paper bags, for example.

They over-burden or even destroy business, creating stiff regulations on manufacturing and small business in the community. They may dictate the number of outlets a business may have in a community, not matter what the population demands. For example, in San Francisco there can only be seven McDonalds.

They can dictate the kind of building materials owners can use in their private home – or whether one can build on their property at all. Then, if they do grant a permit for building, they might not decide to let the property owner acquire water and electricity for the new home – and they may or may not give you a reason for being turned down.

As part of Sustainable health care, they may even dictate that you get the proper exercise – as determined by the government. Again, San Francisco has built a new federal building – the greenest ever built. The elevators will only stop on every third floor so riders are forced to use stairs – for their own health, of course.

These councils fit almost perfectly the definition of a State Soviet: a system of councils that report to an apex council and then implement a predetermined outcome. Soviets are the operating mechanism of a government-controlled economy.

So many things
making **so little sense**:

- EPA drives industries overseas where **pollution increases**
- EPA embraces ethanol while **blaming farming** for pollution
- Master Plans across America **overtly ignore** property rights
- Environmental nooses rob property rights & individual freedoms based on **unsettled science, distorted statistics & exaggerated predictions.**
- Focus on **Social Equity** eclipsing life-liberty property (Why?)
- Municipal Master Plans have become **Manifestos**
- People **in tears** across America

PUBLIC/PRIVATE PARTNERSHIPS

The fourth path to imposing Sustainable Development is Public/Private Partnerships (PPPs). Unfortunately, today, many Conservative/Libertarian organizations are presenting PPPs as free enterprise and a private answer for keeping taxes down by using business to make a better society.

There are certain areas where private business contracts to do jobs such as running school cafeterias through a competitive bid system. That type of arrangement certain does serve the tax payers and provides better services. That's not how PPPs are used though Sustainable Development.

In truth, many PPPs are nothing more than government-sanctioned monopolies in which a few businesses are granted special favors like tax breaks, the power of eminent domain, non-compete clauses and specific guarantees for return on their investments. That means they can fix prices, charge beyond what the market demands, and they can use the power of government to put competition out of business. That is not free enterprise. And it is these global corporations that are pushing the green agenda.

PPPs were the driving force behind the Trans Texas Corridor, using eminent domain to take more than 580,000 acres of private land - sanctioned by the partnership with the Texas government. And PPPs are taking over highways and local water treatment plants in communities across the nation. PPPs in control of the water system can control water consumption – a major part of the Sustainable Development blueprint.

Fueled by federal grant programs through the EPA, the auto industry has produced and forced onto the market "green" cars that no one wants to buy, such as the Chevy Volt. For its part of the partnership, government passed regulations that keep gas prices high to make them more inviting.

The federal government has entered into many partnerships with alternative energy companies in a move to force wind power and solar power on an uninterested public. Again, such industries only exist though the power and of government determined to enforce a certain political agenda. They would never survive in an honest free market.

Using government to ban its own product, General Electric is forcing the mercury-laden green light bulb, costing 5 times the price of incandescent bulbs. Such is the reality of green industry, which depends more on government subsidy and grants than on customers.

The North American Free Trade Agreement (NAFTA) is the root of the "Free Trade" process and the fuel for PPPs between international corporations and government, thereby creating an "elite" class of "connected" businesses – or what Ayn Rand called "the power of pull." Success in the PPP world is not based on quality of product and service, but on who you know in high places. To play ball in the PPP game means accepting the mantra of Sustainable Development and helping to implement it, even if it means going against your own product. That's why Home Depot uses its commercials to oppose cutting down trees and British Petroleum advocates reducing the use of oil.

It is not free enterprise, but a Mussolini-type fascism of government and private industry organized in a near impenetrable force of power. And it's all driven by the Agenda 21 blueprint of Sustainable Development.

ICLEI -Charter 1.7 - Principles

- The Association shall promote, and ask its individual members to adopt, the following Earth Charter Principles to guide local action:
- (6) Prevent harm as the best method of environmental protection and, when knowledge is limited, apply a precautionary approach.
- (7) Adopt patterns of production, consumption, and reproduction that safeguard Earth's regenerative capacities, human rights, and community well-being.
- (9) Eradicate poverty as an ethical, social, and environmental imperative.
- (10) Ensure that economic activities and institutions at all levels promote human development in an equitable and sustainable manner.
- (11) Affirm gender equality and equity as prerequisites to sustainable development and ensure universal access to education, health care, and economic opportunity.
- (14) Integrate into formal education and life-long learning the knowledge, values, and skills needed for a sustainable way of life.

WHAT KINDS OF GROUPS PROMOTE THIS IN THE U.S.A.?

Many Americans ask how dangerous international policies can suddenly turn up in state and local government, all seemingly uniform to those in communities across the nation and around the globe.

The answer – meet ICLEI, a non-profit, private foundation, dedicated to helping locally elected representatives fully implement Agenda 21 in the community. Originally known as the International Council for Local Environmental Initiatives (ICLEI), today the group simply calls itself "ICLEI – Local Governments for Sustainability."

In 1992, ICLEI was one of the groups instrumental in creating Agenda 21. The group's mission is to push local communities to transform the way governments operate, creating a "community plan," creating a wide range of non-elected planning and councils which then impose severe regulations and oversight policies, affecting every homeowner, every business, every school; literally every aspect of the citizen's lives. And it's having tremendous success.

Currently there are over 600 American cities in which ICLEI is being paid dues with tax dollars from city councils to implement and enforce Sustainable Development. ICLEI is there to assure that the mayors keep their promises and meet their goals. Climate change and the goal to cut the communities carbon footprint is, of course, the ICLEI mantra.

Here's just some of the programs ICLEI provides cities and towns, in order to spread their own particular political agenda in the name of "community services" and environmental protection, they include:

• Software programs to help set the goals for community development – which leads to controlling use of private property;

• Access to a network of "Green" experts, newsletters, conferences and workshops – to assure all city employees are in the process;

• Toolkits, online resources, case studies, fact sheets, policy and practice manuals, and blueprints used by other communities;

• Training workshops for staff and elected officials on how to develop and implement the programs;

• And, of course, there's Notification of relevant grant opportunities – this is the important one – money – with severe strings attached.

ICLEI recommends that the community hire a full time "sustainability manager," who, even in small towns, can devote 100% of his time to assure that every nook and corner of the government is on message and under control.

Using environmental protection as the excuse, these programs are about reinventing government with a specific political agenda. ICLEI and others are dedicated to transforming every community in the nation to the Agenda 21 blueprint. .

In addition to ICLEI, groups like the Sierra Club, Nature Conservancy and Audubon Society, NGOs which also helped write Sustainable Development policy have chapters in nearly every city. They know that Congress has written legislation providing grants for cities that implement Sustainablist policy. They agitate to get the cities to accept the grants. If a city rejects the plan, they then agitate to the public, telling them that their elected representatives have cost the city millions in "their" tax dollars. In the end, through such tactics, the NGOs usually get their way.

The NGOs are joined in their efforts by professional planning groups and associations such as the American Planning Association (APA), The Renaissance Planning Group, and the International City/County Management association (ICMA). IN fact there are literally hundreds, if not thousands, of non-profits, NGOs and planning groups living off the grant money, working to enforce Sustainable Development policy at every level of government.

The APA- Professional Planners or
Anti-Capitalist Political Advocacy?

APA embraces ICLEI Programme(s)

1.1 "The built environment is a primary contributor to climate change" ...Business as usual will not suffice"

1.3 Social Equity and Climate Change (& Environmental Justice)

2.4 #6: "Should reduce reliance on coal..."

2.4 #10: Grow food for local consumption (starve the world?)

2.4 #14: Reduce VMT (Vehicle Miles Traveled)

2.4 #15: Cap & Trade for carbon ... needed.

Land Use#15: Create city-funded housing repair programs

Transportation #4: Increase CAFÉ standards

HERE ARE JUST A FEW TO WATCH FOR:

The American Planning Association (APA) is the nation's leading enforcer of Sustainable policy. It came into being in 1978 and can be found in literally every community in the nation. It doesn't have the same open ties to the UN as does ICLEI, but is every bit as involved, if not more so. The APA's "Growing Smart Legislative Guide Book" is found in nearly every university, state and county in the country. It is the planning guide preferred by most urban and regional planners. The American Planning Association is one of many members of the PCSD. They partner with ICLEI & ICMA in the implementation of sustainable development.

ICMA, International City/County Management Association, is an organization of professional local government leaders building sustainable communities worldwide.

ICMA provides technical and management assistance, training, and information resources in the areas of performance measurement, ethics education and training, community and economic development, environmental management, technology, and other topics to its members and the broader local government community.

They are aided in their efforts through such as the U.S. Conference of Mayors, National Governors Association, National League of Cities, the National Association of County Administrators and several more groups that are supposed to represent elected officials.

The Renaissance Planning Group is an urban planning firm. They played a critical role in Florida's "Forever Program". The Forever Program is Florida's premier conservation and recreation lands acquisition program. Florida Forever is the largest public land acquisition program of its kind in the United States. With approximately 9.8 million acres of conservation land in Florida, more than 2.4 million acres were purchased under the Florida Forever and P2000 programs. In 2007, the Virginia state legislature passed HB 3202 mandating that counties with the prescribed growth rate establish high density urban development areas. As a result, to date, 67 counties in the Commonwealth of Virginia are required to establish "urban development areas". The process and proposed land use planning that is being implemented, follows the very same policies called for in Agenda 21's biodiversity plan. This requirement by the state forces local governments to compromise your private property through zoning measures called for in the Smart Growth program for sustainable development.

PlannersNetwork.org

- **STATEMENT OF PRINCIPLES:** *"We believe planning should be a tool for allocating resources... and eliminating the great inequalities of wealth and power in our society... because the free market has proven incapable of doing this."*

The American Farmland Trust (AFT) formed in 1980, works to acquire and control farmer development rights and the purchase of Agriculture Easements which drastically reduce, if not eliminate private ownership of the land.

THE DANGER IS IN THE "PROCESS"

Sustainable policies are being sold universally to the public as a means to protect the environment and control growth. That is simply the excuse for the policies being implemented in its name. The real problem is the "PROCESS" through which Sustainable Development is being forced on unsuspecting citizens. The comprehensive land use plans are being steered by planning groups through manipulation by facilitated stakeholder consensus councils. Though their meetings are "open" to the public, they are void of any public input. The predetermined outcome severely restricts land use and compromises private property ownership in an already distressed market. They answer to no one and they are run by zealots with their own political agenda imposing international laws and regulations. Local homeowners have no say in the process and in most cases are shut out. Sometimes they are literally thrown out of council meetings because they want to discuss how a regulation is going to affect their property or livelihood.

Communities have dealt with local problems for 200 years. Some use zoning, some don't. But locally elected town councils and commissioners, which meet and discuss problems with the citizens, are how this nation was built and prospered. Today, under Sustainable Development, NGOs like ICLEI and the APA move in to establish non-elected boards, councils and regional government bodies.

Despite the Senate's refusal to ratify the Biodiversity Treaty in 1994, the Agenda 21 policies called for by the convention, are being implemented nationwide. No matter where you live, rest assured Agenda 21 policies are being implemented in your community.

Proponents of Agenda 21 and Sustainable Development attempt to ridicule those who oppose the programs as being paranoid radicals who are spreading conspiracy theories about what they call an "obscure 20 year old UN document." Yet, in 2012 the UN sponsored Rio+20, in which 50,000 delegates from around the world to celebrate Agenda 21 and find means to complete its implementation.

Sustainable Development is not about "saving the environment." It is about a revolutionary coup in America. It is about establishing global governance and abandoning the principles of Natural Law on which America was founded.

The politically-based environmental movement provides Sustainablists camouflage as they work to transform the American system of government, justice, and economics. It's a masterful mixture of Socialism, (with its top-down control of the tools of the economy); fascism (where property is owned in name only – with no private control); and Corporatism, (where partnerships between government and private business create government sanctioned monopolies.) Sustainable Development is the worst of both the left and the right. It is bad policy pushed by both liberal and conservatives. It is a new kind of tyranny that, if not stopped, will surely lead all human kind to a new Dark Ages of pain and misery.

 ## What has Sustainability become?

- *Unfortunately, the environmental movement has been hijacked as a convenient excuse to attack capitalism; blame America; transfer wealth; impinge on Constitutional rights; and install a government run socio-economic system.*

- <u>United Nations paradigm:</u> ***Capitalism and private property rights are <u>not sustainable,</u> and pose the single greatest threat to the world's ecosystem and social equity.***

IT'S 1992 ALL OVER AGAIN.
A NEW AGENDA 21 THREATENS OUR WAY OF LIFE

If you had a time machine and could travel back to 1992 as the UN's Earth Summit was underway, your efforts to abort this subversive policy would be aided by all you had experienced in the Orwellian world of "Sustainable Living". You wouldn't have to wonder what the NGOs who created it had in mind. You wouldn't have to trust the news media to provide the details. You would know because you would have lived it. You would know that Nancy Pelosi's open claim that Agenda 21 is a "comprehensive blue print" for the reorganization of human society was true.   And what's more; you don't like it!

We were told, without hesitation, that Agenda 21 was aimed at destroying free enterprise. That it is was a clarion call for humans to live on less and that the Earth could no longer sustain the consumptive appetite of United States of America. They told us, but so many weren't listening. It took over 15 years for many to finally understand the agenda of Agenda 21. By then it was firmly entrenched in every government agency, every community plan, and every school curriculum. So much so that many now say it is impossible to combat. That it's a done deal.

Well, guess what, Agenda 21 is not a done deal and one of the main forces to recognize that fact is the UN itself, along with a mob of enabling Non-Governmental Organizations (NGOs). And because it is not a done deal, they are all planning a new massive gathering to reboot Agenda 21 and force it across the finish line.

Over the weekend of September 25 – 27, 2015, at the United Nations Headquarters in New York City thousands of delegates, UN diplomats, representatives of Non-governmental Organizations, heads of state and the Pope, will converge to present a new fifteen-year plan entitled "Transforming Our World: the 2030 Agenda for Sustainable Development."

Just as in 1992, they are openly telling us what the plan includes and how they intend to put it in force. The preamble to the plan says, "All countries and all stakeholders, acting in collaborative partnership, **WILL** implement this plan." It goes on to say, "We are determined to take the bold and transformative steps which are urgently needed to shift the world onto a sustainable and resilient path. As we embark on this collective journey, we pledge that no one will be left behind." When I read these words I don't glow with anticipation, I bristle with dread.

That, my friends, is a direct challenge and a threat to anyone who dares to disagree with the plan or stand in their way. They promise us that they "WILL" do it and it will be forced on everyone. Our experience with Agenda 21 over the past 23 years tells us what to expect.

Here are the seventeen goals to be presented and what they really mean:

Goal 1. End poverty in all its forms everywhere. The only answer the plan offers for eliminating poverty is redistribution of wealth. The document calls for "equal rights to economic resources." That means government is claiming an absolute power to take away anything that belongs to you to give to whomever it deems more deserving. That is government-sanctioned theft. These are only Band-Aids that solve nothing. Tomorrow those on the bread lines will still need more. There is not a single idea in these plans to give the poor a way to earn their own wealth so they no longer need government hand-outs. The final result; a never ending cycle of poverty that will consume the middle class.

Goal 2. End hunger, achieve food security and improve nutrition and promote sustainable agriculture. UN documents go into great detail on controlling food supplies. They detail enforcing "sustainable farming tactics" which have been proven to force up the cost of food production while decreasing yield. It is basically the old Soviet practice of farm control that turned the bread basket of the world into non productive wasteland. The document details the use of government controlled seed and plant banks... "to ensure access to and fair and equitable

sharing of benefits arising from the utilization of genetic resources and associated traditional knowledge as internation-
ally agreed." In other words, our future food sources will be put
into the hands of politically connected bureaucrats who have
never been on a farm. . Starvation on a massive scale will trim
the population to more sustainable levels.

**Goal 3. Ensure healthy lives and promote well-being of all
at all ages.** This means cradle to grave control over how and
where we live and what we are permitted to eat. The healthy
lives they promote means basically forcing us out of our cars
and into walking and riding bikes as we are relocated into
controlled high rise apartment buildings sanctioned by government. Meat will be out of the question as raising herds is not
considered to be "sustainable. But don't worry. Obamacare for
all will deal with the predictable decline in health that is sure to
follow.

**Goal 4. Ensure inclusive and equitable quality education and
promote lifelong learning opportunities for all.** We have long
known that lifelong learning is the means to continually apply behavior modification practices to assure we maintain the
desired attitudes, values and beliefs to live in a global village

**Goal 5. Achieve gender equality and empower all women and
girls.** The rainbow flag flies as we ignore Shariah law and its
war on women.

**Goal 6. Ensure availability and sustainable management of
water and sanitation.** Ask California how sustainable water
control is working for them as these policies have torn down
water systems and dams to "free the rivers." The original pio-
neers found the land to be a desert. They built a sophisticated
water control system that resulted in an emerald green paradise. Now, as Sustainable policies are being enforced, they are
witnessing the return of the desert, destroying productive
land. Meanwhile, across the nation, the EPA is moving to take
control of all the water in the United States. Control the water,
control the population.

Goal 7. Ensure access to affordable, reliable, sustainable and modern energy for all. Seriously? Their solution is to ban oil and enforce wind and solar power. Every study across the nation and around the world has proven that these "modern" energy sources are unreliable and force up the cost of energy. Some report health problems related to life under the turbines. Moreover, the carnage of the birds and bats that are being chopped up and fried by these "sustainable" energy practices goes against everything environmentalists told us about protecting species.

Goal 8. Promote sustained, inclusive and sustainable economic growth, full and productive employment and decent work for all. One thing our 23 years of Agenda 21 have proven, there is no economic growth. European nations that implemented sustainable energy and water controls guidelines are now dumping those programs as fast as they can to save their economies. And who decides what is "productive" or "decent" work? Do we leave it to the bureaucrats to decide?

Goal 9. Build resilient infrastructure, promote inclusive and sustainable industrialization and foster innovation. Oh come now. Sustainable industrialization means destroyed industry. No real industry can remain in business under a government managed economy with its shifting rules and constant increase in taxes. Government doesn't create industry or prosperity. Our government's real job is to provide protection of the market place so real innovators are free to create new ideas, industries and opportunities. Government itself is a job killer when it gets in the way.

Goal 10. Reduce inequality within and among countries. This is another form of redistribution of wealth that forces industries from first world to third world nations. By using oppressive sustainable policies to drive up production costs, companies are forced to take their factories to the poorer nations. The second trick is to exempt those poorer nations from the very environmental rules and regulations that caused the factories to move in the first place. Can anyone explain how this helps the environment? It doesn't. It simply makes everyone equally poor. This is also an assault on national sovereignty.

Goal 11. Make cities and human settlements inclusive, safe, resilient and sustainable. This is Smart Growth which promises a utopia of families and neighbors playing and working together, riding bikes, walking to work in stress free communities. It really means the end of private property rights, single family homes, and stack and pack high rises where residents are over taxed, over regulated, rents are high and individual thoughts and actions are viewed as a threat to the "well-ordered society." And by the way, the American Planning Association did a study to see if their smart growth plans worked and their own report concluded that Smart Growth doesn't work.

Goal 12. Ensure sustainable consumption and production patterns. What more is there to say? Control from the top down.

Goal 13. Take urgent action to combat climate change and its impacts. Here it is! The root of the entire plan. Climate Change. How many scientific reports do real scientists have to present to show this is the greatest scam ever devised to create a reason for government to control every aspect of our lives? Well, here, let the Global Warming scare mongers tell you their true purpose in their own words: "No matter if the science of global warming is all phony – climate change provides the greatest opportunity to bring about justice and equality in the world." Christine Stewart (former Canadian Minister of the Environment). Justice built on a lie? And here is another quote to make it clear. "We've got to ride this global warming issue. Even if the theory of global warming is wrong, we will be doing the right thing in terms of economic and environmental policy." Timothy Wirth (President, UN Foundation). The end justifies the means! Notice that Mr. Wirth is as concerned with the economy as he is with the environment.

Goal 14. Conserve and sustainably use the oceans, seas and marine resources for sustainable development. Control the water, control society. This one is really aimed at destroying the oil industry in order to enforce wind and solar power. This is the UN pounding its chest to become the central global government it has always sought to be. It has no more right to the seas than it does to the air we breath or the surface of the moon.

Goal 15. Protect, restore and promote sustainable use of terrestrial ecosystems, sustainably manage forests, combat desertification, and halt and reverse land degradation and halt biodiversity loss. Have you been watching the news as the greatest fires in history are destroying millions of acres of forests? Why is this happening? Because of sustainable forest management that refuses to allow the removal of dead trees from the forest floor. This creates a density of combustable material to fuel massively hot and unmanageable fires. If you want to save a forest, send an environmentalist back to his high rise in New York City where he belongs.

Goal 16. Promote peaceful and inclusive societies for sustainable development, provide access to justice for all and build effective, accountable and inclusive institutions at all levels. This is Social Justice which really means social engineering. Have you ever once witnessed an "effective" or "accountable" institution coming out of the United Nations? By its very nature, the UN is unaccountable. Who would be the entity to oversee that accountability? Every one of these programs outlined in the 2030 Agenda creates money, power and unaccountability at every level of government. That is why government is now running out of control and people are feeling so hopeless in trying to deal with their governments. Goal 16 should be named the "Foxes Running the Hen House" goal.

Goal 17. Strengthen the means of implementation and revitalize the global partnership for sustainable development. This means the re-boot of Agenda 21, because that was the original "global partnership." This goal is a call for all of the treaties, plans and schemes devised in the massive UN meetings to be made the law of the globe. It is total global government and it is a sure highway to misery, destruction of human society, individual thought, motivation and dreams.

In 1992 they told us that Agenda 21 was just a suggestion. Today, after experiencing the "wrenching transformation" of our society that Al Gore called for, we know it was much more than that. And we have suffered the consequences as our economy has plummeted, as the middle class is disappearing, jobs are non-existent and the world is in turmoil.

Now the power elite which prey on the poor and helpless are determined to finish the job. They are fast moving toward the goal of eliminating individual nation states; controlling individual actions and wiping private property ownership from the face of the Earth. Their goal is to make us all "equal" in the same chains to assure none of us can disrupt their well ordered utopian nightmare.

Well, now our time machine has brought us back from 1992 to the present. As we disembark, one voice should be ringing in our ears. In clear and concise words we were warned of what Agenda 21 was designed to do. **"Isn't the only hope for the planet that the industrialized nations collapse? Isn't it out responsibility to bring that about?"** The voice belonged to Maurice Strong, Secretary General of the UN Chairman of the Earth Summit as he delivered an official statement.

But here in 2015, the same forces are about to introduce the 2030 Agenda. We have the advantage of knowing what is intended. The 2030 Agenda to "Transform the World" is to be built on the ruins and desolation of a thousand such schemes for control over human life. Each time they have failed to achieve their lofty goals but have brought about a slow decline in liberty and self sufficiency. And each time they have come back with a new "plan." The 2030 Agenda is Agenda 21 re-booted. But this time you and I don't have an excuse to ignore it. We know what it is from the start. Now we have a new opportunity and the obligation to stop it dead in its tracks. We've been given a second chance. Let's not waste it.

GREEN NEW DEAL REVEALS NAKED TRUTH OF AGENDA 21

As a result of my efforts to expose Agenda 21, I've been labeled a conspiracy theorist, scaremonger, extremist, and dangerous nut case. I've been denied access to stages, major news programs, and awarded tin foil hats.

The main weapon to enforce this global Agenda was the threat of Environmental Armageddon, particularly manifested through the charge of man-made global warming, later to conveniently become "climate change."

After trying to hide their real goals, the Agenda 21 globalists have finally exposed the truth.

Enter the Green New Deal.

The Sustainablists have boldly thrown off their cloaking devices and admitted that their goal isn't just "voluntary environmental protection."

Instead, they are now openly revealing that their real goal is socialism and global control, just as I've been warning about for these past twenty seven years.

Now they are determined to take congressional action to finally make it the law of the land.

Here it is step by step:

- I warned that Agenda 21 would control every aspect of our lives, including how and were we live, the jobs we have, the mode of transportation available to us, and even what we eat. The Green New Deal is a tax on everything we do, make, wear, eat, drink, drive, import, export and even breathe.

- In opposing Smart Growth plans in your local community, I said the main goal was to eliminate cars, to be replaced with bikes, walking, and light rail trains. The Green New Deal calls for the elimination of the internal combustion engine. The next step will be to put a ban on the sale of new combustion engines by a specific date and then limiting the number of new vehicles to be sold. Bans on commercial truck shipping will follow. Then they will turn to airplanes, reducing their use. Always higher and higher taxes will be used to get the public to "voluntarily" reduce their use of such personal transportation choices.

- I warned that under Smart Growth programs now taking over every city in the nation that single-family homes are a target for elimination, to be replaced by high-rise stack and pack apartments in the name of reducing energy use. That will include curfews on heating and cooling systems, mandating they be turned off during certain hours. Gradually, energy use of any kind will be continually reduced. The Green New Deal calls for government control of every single home, office and factory to tear down or retrofit them to comply with massive environmental energy regulations.

- I warned that Agenda 21/ Sustainable policy intends to drive those in rural areas off the farms and into the cities where they could be better controlled. Most recently I warned that the beef industry is a direct target for elimination. It will start with mandatory decreases in meat consumption until it disappears form our daily diet. The consumption of dairy will follow. Since the revelation of the Green New Deal, the national debate is now over cattle emissions of methane and the drive to eliminate them from the planet. Controlling what we eat is a major part of the Green New Deal.

- I warned that part of the plan for Agenda 2030 was "Zero Economic Growth." The Green New Deal calls for a massive welfare plan where no one earns more than anyone else. So, where will jobs come from after we have banned most manufacturing, shut down most stores, stopped single-family home construction, closed the airline industry, and severely regulated farms and the entire food industry? This is their answer to the hated free markets and individual choice.

Over these years elected officials have listened to the Sierra Club, the Nature Conservancy, the World Wildlife Fund, ICLEI, the American Planning Association, and many more, as they assured that their plans were just environmental protection - just good policy for future generations. Well, now the truth is right in front of you. There is no question of who and what is behind this. And no doubt as to what the final result will be.

<u>Every industry under attack by this lunacy should now join our efforts to stop it. Cattlemen, farmers, airlines, the auto industry, realtors, tourist industry, the grocers, restaurants, and many more, all will be put out of business – all should now take bold action to immediately kill this plan before it kills your industry. Stomp it so deeply into the ground that no politician will ever dare think about resurrecting it.</u>

For years I've watched politicians smirk, roll their eyes, and sigh whenever the words Agenda 21 were uttered. As George Orwell said, "The further a society drifts from the truth the more it will hate those who speak it".

The Green New Deal has laid bare the horrible reality of my warnings. New York Congresswoman Alexandria Ocasio-Cortez has unwittingly given you and me the weapon we have needed to destroy Agenda 21.

Finally Americans across the country are talking about it. Now many more can see the truth to my dire warnings. **Now is our time to strike with everything we have to stop it.**

Today I stand vindicated in my warnings of where Agenda 21 was truly headed. The Green New Deal is pure Socialism. How far its perpetrators get in enforcing it depends entirely on how hard you and I are willing to fight for freedom. Kill it now or watch freedom die.

HOW TO FIGHT BACK AGAINST SUSTAINABLE DEVELOPMENT

Be aware of the world in which your elected officials live.

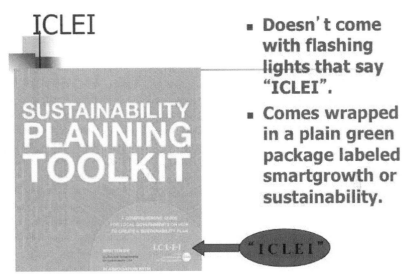

ICLEI

- **Doesn't come with flashing lights that say "ICLEI".**
- **Comes wrapped in a plain green package labeled smartgrowth or sustainability.**

To begin the effort to fight back against Sustainable Development it is vital to first understand the massive structure you are facing. You need to know who the players are and you need to understand the political world your officials are operating in. This may help you to understand that perhaps they aren't all evil globalists, but, perhaps, good people who are surrounded by powers that won't let them see the reality of the policies they are helping to implement. I'm certainly not making excuses for them, but before you rush in and start yelling about their enforcing UN policies on the community, here are some things you should consider.

In most communities, you mayor, city council members and county commissioners are automatically members of national organizations like the National Conference of Mayors, National League of Cities, and the national associations for city council members, and the same for commissioners. Those in the state government also have the National Governors Association and state legislators have their national organization. For the past twenty years or more, each and every one of these national organizations have been promoting Sustainable Development and related policies. The National Mayors Conference and the National Governors Association have been leaders in this agenda, many times working directly with UN organizations to promote the policy. That is the message your local elected leaders hear; from the podium; from fellow officials from other communities; from "experts" they've been told to respect; in committee meetings; from dinner speakers; from literature they are given at such meetings. They are told of legislation that will be soon be implemented, and they are even provided sample legislation to introduce in their communities.

Back home, they are surrounded by a horde of "stakeholder" groups, each promoting a piece of the agenda, be it policies for water control, energy control, development control, specific building materials control, historic preservation and control of "downtown" development, conservation easements and development rights for control of rural property. These groups like ICLEI, the American Planning Association, the Renaissance Planning Group, and many more, are heavily involved with state and federal plans. They arrive in your community with blue prints, state and federal plans, grants and lots of contacts in high places. There are official state and federal programs for "going Green," Comprehensive land use plans, and lots of programs for the kids in the classrooms.

There is also a second horde involved in the Sustainablist invasion – state and federal agency officials including EPA agents; air and water quality agents; Interior Department officials, HUD officials, energy officials, Commerce Department officials, and on and on – all targeting your locally elected officials with policy, money, regulations, reports, special planning boards, meetings, and conferences, all promoting the exact same agenda.

And don't forget the news media, both locally and nationally, also promoting the Sustainablist agenda, attacking anyone not going along, ready to quickly use the "extremist" label against them. The message is clear - Sustainable Development is reality – politically correct, necessary, unquestionable, and it has "consensus."

Is your head spinning yet? Think of the affect all of this has on a poor local official who just thought he would run for office and serve his community. This is his reality. This is what he thinks government is supposed to be because, after all, everyone he is dealing with says so.

Now, as he is surrounded by all of these important, powerful folks, along comes a local citizen who tells him that some guy named Tom DeWeese says all of these programs are from the UN and are taking away our liberty. Who? He said what? Come on, I'm not doing that. And I don't have time to talk about it. I have another meeting to go to.

If we are going to successfully fight Agenda 21, it is vitally important that we all recognize this reality as we plan to deal with it and defeat it. With that in mind, I offer the following ideas.

HOW TO FIGHT BACK

First and foremost, don't try to fight alone. If you try to attend local meetings by yourself you will be ignored. You will need others to plan and implement strategy. You have family and friends. Start with them. Ask them to help look into some local policies. Even if they start off skeptical about your concerns, it won't take them long to see the truth. Check out of there is a local tea party or even a local Republican group. Churches are a target of such policies. Alert people at your church and ask them to help fight back. Find people to help you!

Research: Don't even begin to open up a fight until you know certain details. First, who are the players in your community. What privately funded "stakeholder" groups are there? What is their agenda? What other communities have they operated in? What projects? What results? Who are their members in your community? Are they residents or did they come from "out of town?" (That could prove to be valuable information later in the fight). Finding this information may be the hardest of your efforts. They like to operate out of the spotlight. It's not likely that the town will carry official documentation of who it is working with. It probably will require that you attend lots of meetings and hearings. Take note of who is there and their role. Do this quietly. Don't announce to the community what you are doing. Don't make yourselves a target. You may have to ask questions and that may raise some eyebrows. But stay out of the way as much as possible.

Second, get all the details on the plans your community is working on. Has there already been legislation passed? Most of this information can be found on the town website. Knowing this information will help you put together a plan of action. Once you have it, you can begin to take your fight public.

With the information you have gathered, begin to examine the effect the policies will have on the community and its residents. Find who the victims of the legislation or regulation may be. This will be of great value as you confront city council. People understand victim stories – especially if it is them. It is the best way to undermine the process – and help get people to join your cause.

You will find that Conservation Easements have raised taxes as much of the county land is removed from the tax rolls – someone has to make up for the lost revenue and the payment of easements. Are "stakeholder" groups helping to get landowners to sign up for the easements – and if so – do they get any kind of kickbacks? Who are getting the easements? You may find the rich land owners have found a great loophole to cut their own property taxes as the middle class makes up the short fall. This will help bring usually disinterested people to your cause.

Does the community plan call for reduction of energy use? If so, look for calls for energy audits and taxes on energy use. The audits mean that the government has set a goal to reduce energy use. It may follow that government agents are going to come into your home to inspect your energy use. Then they are going to tell you what must be done in your home to cut usage. That will cost you money. Don't fall for the line that it is all voluntary – to help you save money. They haven't gone to this much trouble to be ignored. Regulations are not voluntary.

These are just a couple of examples of what to look for as you do your research. There are many more, including meters on wells to control water use, smart meters to take away your control of your thermostat; non elected boards and councils to control local development and implement smart growth, leading to population growth; Public/Private Partnerships with local and large corporations to "go Green;" creation of open space; pushing back live stock from streams, enforcing sustainable farming methods that restrict energy and water use in farming practices; and much more. It all leads to higher costs and shortages, in the name of environmental protection and conservation and controlling growth (anti-sprawl, they call it).

Your goal is to stop Sustainable Development in your community. That means a campaign to stop the creation of non-elected regional government councils that are difficult to hold accountable. It means to stop local governments from taking state and federal grants that come with massive strings attached to enforce compliance. And it means you must succeed in removing outsider organizations and Stakeholder groups that are pressuring your elected officials to do their bidding.

Civic Action: Armed with as much information as you can gather (and armed with the ability to coherently discuss its details) you are ready to take your battle to the public. First, it would be better for you to try to discuss it privately with some of your elected officials, especially if you know them. Tell them what you have found and explain why you are opposed. First discuss the effects of the policies on the average citizen. Explain why they are bad. Only very slowly should you bring the conversation around to the origin of such polices - Agenda 21 and the UN. Don't start there. It is important that you build the case to show that these policies are not local, but part of a national and international agenda. If this conversation does not go well (and it probably won't) then you have to take it to the next level – to the public.

Begin a two fold campaign. First, write a series of letters to the editor for the local newspaper. Make sure that you are not alone. Coordinate your letters with others who will also write letters to back up and support what you have written. These will generate more letters from others, some for your position and other against you. Be prepared to answer those against you as they are probably written by those "Stakeholders" who are implementing the policies in the first place. This may be a useful place for you to use what you've learned about these groups to discredit them.

Second, begin to attend Council meetings and ask questions. The response from the council members will determine your next move. If you are ignored and your questions met with silence or hostility, prepare a news release detailing your questions and the background you have as to why you asked those questions. Pass the news release out to the people at the next meeting as well as the news media. Attend the next meeting and the next demanding answers. Be sure to organize people to come with you. Don't try this alone. If necessary, have demonstrators outside city hall carrying signs or handing out flyers with the name and picture of the officials who won't answer your questions along with the question you asked – including the details you have about the policy.

The point in all of this is to make the issue public. Take away their ability to hide the details from the public. Expose the hoards of outsiders who are dictating policy in your community. Force the people you elected to deal with YOU – not the army of self-appointed "stakeholders" and government officials. Shine a very right spotlight on the roaches under the rock.

If the newspaper is with you, great, but you will probably find it working with the other side. It may be difficult to get a fair shake in the newspaper or on radio. That's why you deliver your news releases to both the media and the public. Get signs, and flyers in stores if necessary. And keep it up for as long as it takes. Don't stop the public demonstration until you had acquired victory, or at least started a public debate.

The final step is to use the energy you have created to run candidates for office against those who have ignored and fought you. Ultimately, that is the office holders worst nightmare and may be the most effective way to get them to respond and serve their constituents.

NEW TACTIC

As mentioned in the beginning, over the past couple of years, as we've educated people on Agenda 21 and its UN origins, the natural reaction by concerned citizens and activists has been to rush into city hall and accuse their elected representatives of implementing international policies on the town. This has, of course, been met with skepticism and ridicule on the part of some of the elected officials (egged on by the NGO stakeholder groups and planning organizations). Today, the promoters of Agenda 21, including ICLEI and the American Planning Association (APA) have worked overtime to paint our movement as crazed conspiracy theorists wearing tin foil hats and hearing voices.

So, it's time to change tactics.

Here is an undeniable fact: Agenda 21/Sustainable Development cannot be enforced without usurping or diminishing private property rights. So, we need to begin to challenge the plans that affect private property rights. However, as we move in that direction, we must have a clear understanding of what property rights are. Many people today have little or varying ideas of property rights. Forty years ago people understood things like "No Trespassing," "My home is my castle," and "step across that line and suffer the consequences." Such ideas today seem quaint and antiquated to many, especially with government invading private property at will. Sometimes, in order to purchase property or to get access to services, we sign documents that say government or utility agents are free to come on our property at will. The idea of "Keep Out" is almost unheard of. However, to demand that your private property be honored and protected a definition must be established before you start the effort.

Attached is a document designed to provide such a definition and understanding of what we mean by private property rights. It is based on the ideas of John Locke, the man who greatly influenced our Founding Fathers including Thomas Jefferson. So using such definitions should fit in with the Founder's intent as the nation's laws on property were written.

Second, once that definition has been established it can be used as a guideline for drafting legislation and resolutions in state legislatures and city hall. It must also be the guideline for the establishment of property rights councils.

Third, please find two more documents, one entitled "Resolution to Protect Citizen's Property Rights," the other "Planner's Pledge to Uphold and Protect Citizen's Property Rights." These documents are guidelines. Change them to fit your needs. I do not present these Resolutions as legal documents such as a contract, though some try to turn them into that. If that is your plan, go ahead and make it so. But we see them as a statement, a way to draw out your elected officials.

The Resolution is for signatures by your elected representatives. The other is to present to your elected representatives to ask them to have the planners that they hire sign it. Use either or both as you wish. The Resolution automatically creates a friction with the elected officials. If you have a strong, positive relationship with them you may not want to force it on them. Then you would want to politely present the Planners Pledge to ask them to have the planners sign it. Or you may want to present both and demand that both entities sign their respective documents.

The way to use it is this: As you stand in front of the elected officials at their regular meeting, ask them simply, "As you bring these planners into our community and begin to implement their programs, what guarantees do I have that you will protect my private property rights?" At this point you haven't mentioned Agenda 21, and you haven't attacked planning. You are simply asking a non-combative question. They will assure you that they are in full support of protecting private property. And then you say, "Well, I'm happy to hear that. But, I would really like to have that in writing." And you present the resolution to them. If you can read it aloud to the meeting, so much the better. They may say they need to take it under consideration and will get back to you. Fine. Make sure you are back at the next meeting to ask about it. If they say "No." You simply ask "Why?" and take it from there.

Do not attempt this alone. The key to this effort is persistence and organization. If they have refused to sign it then you need 5 or 10 people to stand up and ask why. You need to escalate this at each meeting until it becomes a public issue - "Why won't your elected officials sign a simple document that says they will protect your private property rights? What are they hiding in the plans they are presenting to us?" This can and will lead to protests, letters to the editor and other media available to you. Put the elected officials' names on signs carried by protestors who are rallying outside the next council or planning meeting. Make them the issue. What you are really doing is laying the ground work for a campaign to defeat them in the next election.

It is also important to do research into what planning groups, non-governmental organizations (NGO's) federal grants and agencies may be involved in the process. All of them have a background. Find out who they are and what they have done in the past in other communities and present that info to your fellow citizens as a warning of what is to come. I recommend that you create a "rapid response team" to be prepared to immediately respond in the media to anything they do. Make them scared to act.

ICLEI / Agenda 21 dogma

- **Elevates nature above man**
- **40 chapters of socialist control mechanisms**
- **Human settlements;**
- **Educate with environment as central principle**
- **Unsustainable- Ski Lodges, Golf courses, asphalt, fossil fuels, consumerism, irrigation, commercial farms, livestock grazing**

FIGHTING ICLEI

If ICLEI is in your city, the details about Agenda 21 and the UN connection is easier. Your community is paying them dues with your tax dollars. Here is how to handle them: if your council derides your statements that their policies come from the UNs Agenda 21, simply print out the home page from ICLEI's web site – www.iclei.org. This will have all of the UN connections you've been talking about, in ICLEI's own words. Pass out the web page copies to everyone in the chamber audience and say to your elected officials, "don't call me a radical simply for reporting what ICLEI openly admits on its own web site. I'm just the one pointing it out – you are the ones who are paying our tax dollars to them."Then demand that those payment stop. You have proven your case.

STOPPING CONSENSUS MEETINGS

Most public meetings are now run by trained and highly paid facilitators whose jobs is to control the meeting and bring it to a preplanned conclusion. If he is good at his job, the facilitator can actually make the audience think the "consensus" they have reached on and issue or proposal is actually their idea.

This is how Sustainable Development is being implemented across the nation, especially in meetings or planning boards that are advertised as open to the public. They really don't want you there and the tactic is used to move forward in full view of the public without them knowing what is happening. There is nothing free or open about the consensus process. It is designed to eliminate debate and close discussion.

To bust up the process you must never participate, even to answer a question. To do so allows the facilitator to make you part of the process. Instead, you must control the discussion. Here is a quick suggestion on how to foul up the works. Never go alone to such a meeting. You will need at least three people – the more the better. Do not sit together. Instead, fan out in the room in a triangle formation. Know ahead of time the questions you want to ask: Who is the facilitator? What is his association with the organizers? Is he being paid? Where did these programs (being proposed) come from? How are they to be funded?
One question to ask over and over again, both at facilitated meetings and city council meetings, is this: "With the imple-mentation of this policy, tell me a single right or action I have on my property that doesn't require your approval or involve-ment. What are my rights as a property owner?" Make them name it. You will quickly see that they too understand there are no property rights left in America.

By asking these questions you are putting his legitimacy in question, building suspicion among the rest of the audience, destroying his authority. He will try to counter, either by pa-tronizing and humoring you, at first, or, then becoming hostile, moving to have you removed as a disruptive force. That's where the rest of your group comes in. They need to back you up, demand answers to your questions. If you have enough people in the room you can cause a major disruption, making it impos-sible for the facilitator to move forward with his agenda. Do not walk out and leave the room to him. Stay to the end and make him shut down the meeting.

IN CONCLUSION...

These suggestions on how to fight back are, admittedly, very basic and elementary. They are meant only to be a guideline. You will have to do your homework and adapt these tactics to your local situation. These tactics are designed to create controversy and debate to force the Agenda 21 issue out of the secret meetings and into public debate where they belong. Many of these same tactics can be used at all levels of government, right up and into the state legislature. Our plan is to demand answers from elected officials who want to ignore us. They must be taught that such actions have consequences.

As we learn new, successful tactics, I'll share them with activists across the nation. The Americans Policy Center is now a partner in a new effort to create tactics and provide education to activists called Sustainable Freedom Lab. Here activists across the nation can share their findings, successful tactics and research with the rest of the movement. The website is www.sustainablefreedomlab.com.

The exciting news is that, finally, Americans are starting to understand that Agenda 21 is destroying our nation and they are beginning to fight back. The battle to stop the UN's Agenda 21 is ragging on the local level across the nation.

PROPERTY RIGHTS DEFINED

Experts have left a clear understanding of what property means:

"Property is defined by (Washington) state law. Board of Regents v. Roth, 408 U.S. 564, 92 S. Ct. 2701, 2709, 33 L. Ed. 2d 548 (1972). Our state, and most other states, define property in an extremely broad sense."

- From "Fifth Amendment" treatise by State Supreme Court Justice Richard B. Sanders (12/10/97)

"Property in a thing consists not merely in its ownership and possession, but in the unrestricted right of use, enjoyment, and disposal. Anything which destroys any of the elements of property, to that extent, destroys the property itself. The substantial value of property lies in its use. If the right of use be denied, the value of the property is annihilated and ownership is rendered a barren right."

"The moment the idea is admitted into society that property is not as sacred as the law of God, and that there is not a force of law and public justice to protect it, anarchy and tyranny commence."

- President John Adams

"Ultimately, property rights and personal rights are the same thing."

- President Calvin Coolidge

"If you don't have the right to own and control property then you are property.

- Wayne Hage, rancher

Private Property Rights means:

• The owner's exclusive authority to determine how private property is used;

• The owner's peaceful possession, control, and enjoyment of his/her legally purchased, deededprivate property;

• The owner's ability to make contracts to sell, rent, or give away all or part of the legally purchased/deeded private property;

• That local, city, county, state, and federal governments are prohibited from exercising eminent domain for the sole purpose of acquiring legally purchased/deeded private property so as to resell to a private interest or generate revenues;

• That no local, city, county, state, or federal government has the authority to impose directives, ordinances, fees, or fines regarding aesthetic landscaping, color selections, tree and plant preservation, or open spaces on legally purchased/deeded private property;

• That no local, city, county, state or federal government shall implement a land use plan that requires any part of legally purchased/deeded private property be set aside for public use or for a Natural Resource Protection Area directing that no construction or disturbance may occur;

• That no local, city, county, state, or federal government shall implement a law or ordinance restricting the number of dwellings that may be placed on legally purchased/deeded private property;

• That no local, city, county, state, or federal government shall alter or impose zoning restrictions or regulations that will devalue or limit the ability to sell legally purchased/deeded private property;

That no local, city, county, state, or federal government shall limit profitable or productive agriculture activities by mandating and controlling what crops and livestock are grown on legally purchased/deeded private property;

• That no local, city, county, state, or federal government representatives or their assigned agents may enter private property without the written permission of the property owner or is in possession of a lawful warrant from a legitimate court of law. This includes invasion of property rights and privacy by government use of unmanned drone flights.

PROTECTING YOUR PROPERTY RIGHTS

While there are many forms of property, for the purposes of this brief pamphlet, we are only going to discuss real estate property, the value, how easy it is to lose them and how to protect your property rights. This is only a guide. Always consult your real estate attorney before taking any action that may risk your property rights.

WHAT IS MEANT BY MY REAL ESTATE PROPERTY?

When you own a home your property consists of the land agreed to in your purchase, the natural resources, minerals, crops, water and any buildings on your land.

WHAT ARE MY PROPERTY RIGHTS?

You have the right to sell, transfer, lease, and develop your property. For instance, you can build a swing set, remove a tree or build a swimming pool. The freedom to make these changes increases your land's value to you and to buyers.

WHO PROTECTS MY PROPERTY RIGHTS?

There are laws that protect these rights and prevent others from confiscating or using your property without your express permission. The US Constitution protects your property rights in the 5th amendment.

WHY ARE MY REAL ESTATE PROPERTY RIGHTS SO IMPORTANT?

Real estate ownership is the main way Americans save money and accumulate wealth. They use real estate to improve their lives, start businesses, and leave money to their children. Homeowners tend to protect their surrounding environment and build more stability for their own future. When people lose all or part of their property rights, they often lose their greatest source of wealth and well-being.

HOW ARE MY PROPERTY RIGHTS LOST OR REDUCED?
EMINENT DOMAIN:

The state can seize your private property without your consent to create public facilities, highways, and railroads and for the purpose of economic development or revenue enhancement. You are entitled to compensation, but the agency acquiring your property calculates the payment, which is often inadequate.

GOVERNMENT REGULATIONS:

Governments through federal agencies including the EPA and HUD impose regulations through the Clean Water Act, Endangered Species Act and many others that limit or erase your property rights.

STATE REGULATIONS:

States create urban growth boundaries and increase the cost of services beyond those boundaries to force growth into smaller more densely populated areas . This makes your rural property less valuable and more expensive to maintain, diminishing your wealth.

LOCAL PLANNING:

Local zoning ordinances can infringe upon your property rights and increase the costs of ownership rendering your property less desirable and therefore less valuable when you go to sell it or borrow money against it.

CONSERVATION EASEMENTS:

Some farmers sell the development rights to their property to a government agency or land trust in exchange for cash or tax benefits. These are called 'conservation easements.' While they appear good at first, the landowner becomes subservient to the trust, must obey shifting regulations, and enhanced 'best practices' mandated by the new development rights' holder. Often these practices become too costly, forcing the landowner to sell their property, often to the same agency or land trust that purchased the conservation easement in the first place.

FEDERAL GRANT MONEY:

While grant money from the EPA, HUD and DOT can be enticing, it frequently comes with strings attached that mandate how the money will be used and, in turn, how it can control your community and your property.

REGIONALIZATION:

Regionalization rolls up your community into a larger regional planning area that shrinks your influence over what regulations are passed and reduces the authority of local public officials to act on your behalf to protect your property rights.

DOES THIS MEAN ALL PLANNING AND ZONING REGULATIONS ARE BAD?

No. It means many plans contain regulations that can be damaging to your property rights. Also, some officials agree to regional, rather than local planning. Good planning does not have to mean the loss of property rights.

HOW CAN I PROTECT MY PROPERTY RIGHTS FROM POOR PLANNING AND REGIONALIZATION?

• Understand that most officials do not want to steal your property rights. In the zeal to go 'sustainable', many people look at the environment, the region and the globe first and your property rights last.

• If regionalization is proposed, read all information and find out what happens to local authority once the region is formed. Check how many unelected bureaucrats become the real decision-makers. Regardless of the colorful sales bulletins and friendly environmental talk, regional planning trumps the rights of local citizens. Local rule is the only way to protect personal property rights.

• Recognize that planners, even those from federal agencies, are in your community to sell a plan. They will present vivid before and after pictures of your community that will compel you to want to act right away. Don't. If the plan is that good, it will wait. Most plans end up looking very similar. While nearly all planners talk about public agreement, the reality is 97-99% of citizens are never involved in the planning process. Their property rights are still affected.

• Most importantly, insist that any planners working for your community must sign an agreement committing them to protect your property rights during the planning process. In the event there are infringements on your property rights, they must inform you and offer you the opportunity to opt out.

RESOLUTION TO PROTECT
CITIZEN'S PROPERTY RIGHTS

The undersigned elected officials and/or community planners officially engaged to create planning programs for the community of _____ do hereby agree to the following:

• That planning involves and affects regulation of private property rights.
• That individual property ownership constitutes an asset of unique value, as well as the foundation of individual liberty for American citizens.

Recognizing that value, we agree that all citizen's private property rights shall be placed in the highest priority of consideration during the planning and zoning process; and,

In the event that any part of the planning and zoning process or recommendations resulting from the process shall potentially negatively impact any property rights, property owners or the value of their private property, those affected property owners shall:

a) Be provided full, timely disclosure notifying the property owner or owners of the potential that their private property rights may in some way be infringed or the value of their private property may be thereby affected, and,
b) Be provided full disclosure outlining the rights to be infringed upon, and
c) Be provided an opportunity to opt-out of any rights' infringing regulation or policy.

In the event of property loss or usage by the private land owner due to planning restrictions or amount equal to the fractional fair market loss of the original value of his property as a result of such zoning or other related restrictions on the fair legal use of his property.

Further, affected property owners shall be notified of the potential impairment to their rights and their individual written approval required before engaging in any of the following:

a) Reconfiguration of zoning that intensifies or in any way adds restrictions to existing rights,
b) Implementation of conservations easements or Trading of Development Rights,
c) Acceptance of grant money by the above named government entity or their assigned planners, whether from non-profit organizations, governmental or private funding sources.

Finally, it is agreed that no government representatives or their assigned planning agents, will come on to private property for any planning purpose without the written consent of the owner.

Signed: (Elected Officials)

_____

_____

Signed: (Planning Firm)

_____

_____

Made in the USA
Middletown, DE
05 November 2021

51046928R10040